SELECTIONS FROM
The Piano Rolls

GERSHWIN® is a registered trademark of Gershwin Enterprises
GEORGE GERSHWIN® and IRA GERSHWIN®
are registered service marks of Gershwin Enterprises
All Rights Reserved

Transcribed by: GEORGE LITTEREST with *FINALE*®
Edited and Arranged by: ARTIS WODEHOUSE
Project Manger: TONY ESPOSITO

FINALE® is a registered trademark of CODA Music Technology
All Rights Reserved   Used by Permission

Exclusively Distributed By

ISBN-13: 978-0-89724-980-5

Contents

KICKIN' THE CLOUDS AWAY

Words by IRA GERSHWIN
and B.G. DeSYLVA

Music by GEORGE GERSHWIN
Piano Roll Performance by GEORGE GERSHWIN®
Transcribed by GEORGE LITTERST with FINALE®
Edited and Arranged by ARTIS WODEHOUSE

14

DRIFTING ALONG WITH THE TIDE

Words by ARTHUR JACKSON

Music by GEORGE GERSHWIN
Piano Roll Performance by GEORGE GERSHWIN®
Transcribed by GEORGE LITTERST with FINALE®
Edited and Arranged by ARTIS WODEHOUSE

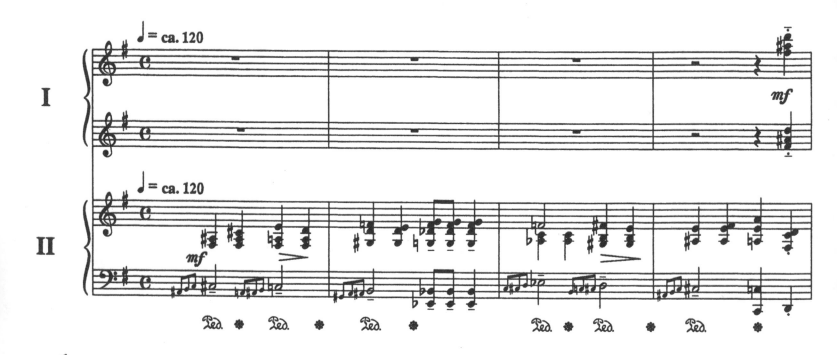

SO AM I

Music and Lyrics by GEORGE GERSHWIN and IRA GERSHWIN
Piano Roll Performance by GEORGE GERSHWIN®
Transcribed by GEORGE LITTERST with FINALE®
Edited and Arranged by ARTIS WODEHOUSE

SWANEE

Words by IRVING CAESAR

Music by GEORGE GERSHWIN
Piano Roll Performance by GEORGE GERSHWIN®
Transcribed by GEORGE LITTERST with FINALE®
Edited and Arranged by ARTIS WODEHOUSE

SWEET AND LOW-DOWN

Music and Lyrics by GEORGE GERSHWIN and IRA GERSHWIN
Piano Roll Performance by GEORGE GERSHWIN®
Transcribed by GEORGE LITTERST with FINALE®
Edited and Arranged by ARTIS WODEHOUSE

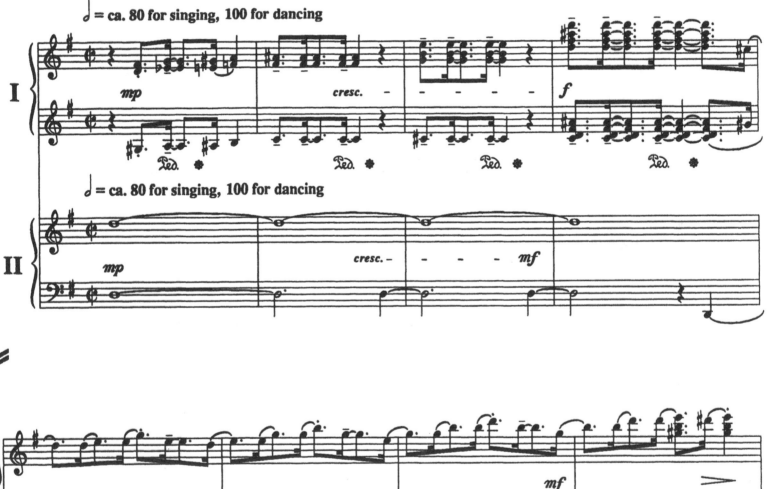

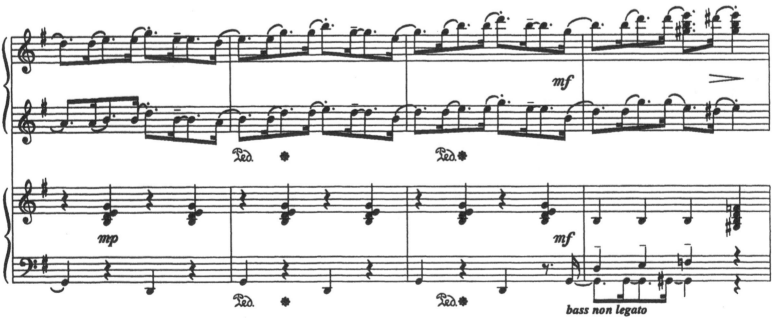

THAT CERTAIN FEELING

Music and Lyrics by GEORGE GERSHWIN and IRA GERSHWIN
Piano Roll Performance by GEORGE GERSHWIN®
Transcribed by GEORGE LITTERST with FINALE®
Edited and Arranged by ARTIS WODEHOUSE

Artis Wodehouse

Pianist and scholar Artis Wodehouse has established herself as a specialist in historic sound recordings. She received her DMA in piano performance practice from Stanford University, where she began using early recordings to study 19th century piano performance style. Since 1982, she has been involved with the works of George Gershwin, transcribing and performing music issued on commercial disc recordings. "Wodehouse is something of a pioneer in research on early sound recordings," wrote the New York Times of her 1987 Gershwin recital at Merkin Hall. "Her transcription of the song improvisations recorded by the composer in the 1920s are delightful."

In 1989-90 Wodehouse received an NEH grant to study Gershwin's approximately 130 piano rolls. Widely scattered among various public and private collections, the rolls first had to be located and analyzed. Wodehouse then began the process of playing them on a rare 1911 Pianola, which was placed in front of a Yamaha Disklavier. The Disklavier recorded the rolls, and Wodehouse edited the resulting computer disks to achieve performances that resembled Gershwin's recorded interpretations. These disks were played back for "Gershwin Plays Gershwin" (Elektra Nonesuch 79287) on a nine-foot Disklavier grand piano, with Wodehouse and producer Max Wilcox overseeing the final recording.